MW00861032

# PIECES D'ORGUE

Consistantes en deux Messes
l'Vne à l'usage ordinaire des Paroisses,
Pour les Festes Solemnelles.
L'Autre propre pour les Conuents de Religieux,
et Religieuses.

COMPOSÉES PAR F. COVPERIN, Sr. DE CROVILLY

ORGANISTE DE St. GERVAIS.

Le Prix de chacune Messe iiii Livres.

A PARIS.

chez l'Autheur proche le Grand Portail
de l'Eglise St. Geruais.

AVEC PRIVILEGE DV ROY.

Engraved title page of the original publication, 1690
(Bibliothèque Inguimbertine de Carpentras, France)

# TWO MASSES FOR ORGAN

*Mass for the Parishes*

*Mass for the Convents*

## FRANÇOIS COUPERIN

DOVER PUBLICATIONS, INC.
New York

*Copyright*

Copyright © 1994 by Dover Publications, Inc.
All rights reserved under Pan American and International Copyright Conventions.

*Bibliographical Note*

This Dover edition, first published in 1994, is a republication in one volume of two works originally published separately in earlier authoritative editions. The Dover edition adds: a new note on organ registration, a glossary of French terms in the music, and a contents list and sectional headings that combine new English translations with the original French organ terms.

For his note on organ registration and other valuable suggestions, we are grateful to Gregory Eaton, Lecturer in Church Music at the General Theological Seminary in New York, and Director of Music of the Church of St. Ann & the Holy Trinity, Brooklyn.

*Library of Congress Cataloging-in-Publication Data*

Couperin, François, 1668–1733.
    [Pièces d'orgue. Messe à l'usage ordinaire des paroisses]
    Two masses for organ / François Couperin.
    p. of music.
    Reprints: "Originally published separately in earlier authoritative editions, n.d."
    Contents: Mass for the parishes—Mass for the convents.
    ISBN 0-486-28285-6 (pbk.)
    1. Organ masses.  I. Couperin, François, 1668–1733. Pièces d'orgue. Messe pour les couvents.
M14.3.C79P506   1994                               94-18596
                                                          CIP
                                                          M

Manufactured in the United States of America
Dover Publications, Inc., 31 East 2nd Street, Mineola, N.Y. 11501

# CONTENTS

Registration Suggestions                                                                 vii

Glossary of French Terms in the Music                                                     viii

Mass for the Parishes (1690)                                                              1
*[Messe à l'usage ordinaire des Paroisses, pour les Festes Solemnelles]*

    [I]    Plainchant of the First Kyrie, *en Taille*    3

    [II]    Fugue on the *Jeux d'Anches* (2nd Kyrie)    4

    [III]    *Récit de Cromorne* (3rd Kyrie)    6

    [IV]    Dialogue on the *Trompette* and *Cromorne* (4th Kyrie)    8

    [V]    Plainchant (5th and last Kyrie)    10

    [VI]    *Plein Jeu* (Et in terra pax)    11

    [VII]    Little Fugue on the *Cromorne* (Gloria, 2nd verse)    12

    [VIII]    Duet on the *Tierces* (Gloria, 3rd verse)    13

    [IX]    Dialogue between the *Trompettes, Clairon* and *Tierces* of the *Grand Clavier* and the *Bourdon* with the *Larigot* of the *Positif* (Gloria, 4th verse)    15

    [X]    Trio for Two Manuals on the *Cromorne* and the *Basse de Tierce* (Gloria, 5th verse)    18

    [XI]    *Tierce en Taille* (Gloria, 6th verse)    20

    [XII]    Dialogue on the *Voix Humaine* (Gloria, 7th verse)    22

    [XIII]    Trio Dialogue of the *Cornet* and the *Tierce* (Gloria, 8th verse)    25

    [XIV]    Dialogue on the *Grands Jeux* (Gloria, 9th and last verse)    28

    [XV]    Offertory on the *Grands Jeux*    30

    [XVI]    Plainchant of the First Sanctus, in Canon    37

    [XVII]    *Récit de Cornet* (2nd Sanctus)    38

    [XVIII]    Benedictus, *Cromorne en Taille*    39

    [XIX]    Plainchant of the Agnus Dei, alternately *en Basse* and *en Taille*    41

    [XX]    Dialogue on the *Grands Jeux* (3rd Agnus)    43

    [XXI]    Deo Gratias, *Petit Plein Jeu*    45

Mass for the Convents (1690)                                                              47
*[Messe pour les Convents de Religieux et Religieuses]*

    [I]    *Plein Jeu* (1st Kyrie)    49

    [II]    Fugue on the *Trompette* (2nd Kyrie)    50

    [III]    *Récit de Cromorne* (3rd Kyrie)    52

    [IV]    Trio for Two Manuals on the *Cromorne* and the *Basse de Tierce* (4th Kyrie)    54

    [V]    Dialogue between the *Trompette* of the *Grand Clavier* and the *Montre, Bourdon* and *Nazard* of the *Positif* (5th and last Kyrie)    56

[VI]    *Plein Jeu* (Gloria, 1st verse)    58

[VII]   Little Fugue on the *Cromorne* (Gloria, 2nd verse)    59

[VIII]  Duet on the *Tierces* (Gloria, 3rd verse)    60

[IX]    *Basse de Trompette* (Gloria, 4th verse)    62

[X]     *Cromorne sur la Taille* (Gloria, 5th verse)    64

[XI]    Dialogue on the *Voix Humaine* (Gloria, 6th verse)    66

[XII]   Trio: Upper voices on the *Tierce* and bass on the *Trompette* (Gloria, 7th verse)    68

[XIII]  *Récit de Tierce* (Gloria, 8th verse)    70

[XIV]   Dialogue on the *Grands Jeux* (Gloria, last verse)    72

[XV]    Offertory on the *Grands Jeux*    74

[XVI]   First Sanctus, *Plein Jeu*    80

[XVII]  *Récit de Cornet* (2nd Sanctus)    81

[XVIII] Elevation, *Tierce en Taille*    82

[XIX]   Agnus Dei, *Plein Jeu*    85

[XX]    Dialogue on the *Grands Jeux* (Conclusion of the Agnus Dei)    86

[XXI]   Deo Gratias, *Petit Plein Jeu*    88

# REGISTRATION SUGGESTIONS

French Classic practices of organ registration were based upon an additive principle, starting with the foundation (whether 8′ or 16′) and adding the registers above in order. Thus, most of the following suggestions assume that there is no "gapped" registration—for example, 8′ + 2′ or 8′ + 4′ + 1⅓′. However, the foundation need not always be a flue stop: a solo combination of 8′ Cromorne, 4′ flute and 2⅔′ Nasard is appropriate and pleasing. This principle admits the possibility of omitting mutations in register-building, but not the even octaves.

The *Jeux Doux* was usually either flute 8′ or flutes 8′ & 4′, depending upon balance with the solo to be accompanied.

Solo combinations, when based upon a reed stop, varied according to the sound of individual organs. In some cases, no flues were added; in others, 8′ and/or 4′ might be added. Certain combinations, however, were considered *de rigueur*:

> *Récit de Nasard*: Flutes 8′ & 4′, Nasard 2⅔′
> *Récit de Tierce*: Flutes 8′, 4′ & 2′, Nasard 2⅔′, Tierce 1⅗′
> *Récit de Larigot*: Flutes 8′, 4′ & 2′, Larigot 1⅓′
> *Grosse Tierce*: Bourdon 16′, Flutes 8′ & 4′, Grosse Nasard 5⅓′ (optional), Grosse Tierce 3⅕′

The *Combinaisons des Jeux* were constructed as follows:

The GRAND PLEIN JEU consisted of the Bourdon (or Montre) 16′, Montres (Principals) 8′, 4′, 2′ and mixtures of both the Grand-Orgue and the Positif. The manuals were coupled.

The PLEIN JEU omitted the 16′ register of the Grand Plein Jeu. Plainchant melodies in the Pedal were played on the Flûte 8′ with a Trompette or Cromorne 8′.

The PETIT PLEIN JEU omitted the mixtures of either the Grand-Orgue or Positif, and entirely excluded the Cymbales or other high mixtures.

For the GRAND JEUX there were two basic possibilities, but both must be modified to suit individual instruments and acoustics. The basic scheme uses the 8′ flute, Montres 4′ & 2′, Cornets, and the 8′ (& 4′) Trompette (or Cromorne) of both the Grand-Orgue and Positif, which are coupled together. The Récit, when present, should have the Cornet, with or without the Cromorne, as desired. The Pedal should have the Grand-Orgue and Positif coupled in, without any independent 16′ registers. The usual variation on this was to add the 16′ Bourdon or Montre, and the Grosse Nasard and Grosse Tierce when available. The Pedal may then include 16′ tone.

As with all organ registration, these suggestions must be tempered by the registers available on a specific instrument, as well as acoustics, touch and related considerations.

GREGORY EATON

# GLOSSARY OF FRENCH TERMS IN THE MUSIC

*continuation*, continuation

*fin*, end

*Grand Jeu précédent à chaque clavier*, draw the reeds on each manual

*lentement*, slowly

*les 2 mains et les 2 pieds ensemble*, both hands and both feet together

*les 2 mains sur* [*le Grand Clavier, etc.*], both hands on [the Grand Clavier, etc.]

*main droite*, right hand

*main gauche*, left hand

*majeur*, major [key]

*mineur*, minor [key]

*une octave plus bas*, one octave lower

# MASS FOR THE PARISHES

*[Messe à l'usage ordinaire des Paroisses,*
*pour les Festes Solemnelles]*

(1690)

# [I] Plainchant of the First Kyrie
## *en Taille*

3

# [II] Fugue on the *Jeux d'Anches*
## (2nd Kyrie)

# [III] *Récit de Cromorne*

## (3rd Kyrie)

G.O.: Bourdon 8, Flûte 4.
P.: Cromorne.

Jeu doux

Chromhorne

# [IV] Dialogue on the *Trompette* and *Cromorne*

## (4th Kyrie)

G.O. : Trompette
P. : Cromorne

Les 2 mains sur le grand Clavier

# [V] Plainchant
## (5th and last Kyrie)

Grand Plein Jeu.
Péd.: Anches 8-4

Pedalle

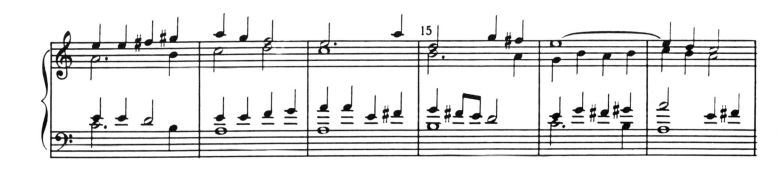

# [VI] *Plein Jeu*

## (Et in terra pax)

# [VII] Little Fugue on the *Cromorne*
## (Gloria, 2nd verse)

[P.: Cromorne, Bourdon 8, Prestant 4.]

# [VIII] Duet on the *Tierces*

## (Gloria, 3rd verse)

G.O.: Bourdons 16,8, Flûte 4, Grosse Tierce 3 ⅕
P.: Cornet décomposé.

# [IX] Dialogue
## between the *Trompettes*, *Clairon* and *Tierces* of the *Grand Clavier* and the *Bourdon* with the *Larigot* of the *Positif*

### (Gloria, 4th verse)

# [X] Trio for Two Manuals
## on the *Cromorne* and the *Basse de Tierce*
### (Gloria, 5th verse)

P.: Cromorne
G.O.: Cornet décomposé

# [XI] *Tierce en Taille*

## (Gloria, 6th verse)

P.: Bourdon 8, Flûte 4.
G.O.: Cornet décomposé.
Péd.: Flûte 8.

Fond d'orgue (P.)

Pedalle de flute.

Tierce (G.O.)

# [XII] Dialogue on the *Voix Humaine*
## (Gloria, 7th verse)

Les 2 mains sur la Voix humaine.

# [XIII] Trio Dialogue of the *Cornet* and the *Tierce*

## (Gloria, 8th verse)

Écho : Cornet
  P.: Bourdon 8, Nasard, Tierce.
G.O.: Bourdon 8.
Péd .: Flûte 8.

# [XIV] Dialogue on the *Grands Jeux*

## (Gloria, 9th and last verse)

G.O.: Montre **8**, Bourdon **8**, Prestant **4**, Doublette **2**,
      Cornet, Trompette, Clairon.
P.: Bourdon **8**, Prestant **4**, Doublette **2**.
R.: Cornet.
    Claviers accouplés.

Positif.

Continuation du Positif.

Les 2 mains sur le Grand Clavier.

G.C.

# [XV] Offertory on the *Grands Jeux*

G.O.: Grand Jeu.
P.: Cromorne.
R.: Cornet.
Péd.: Flûtes 8-4.

Grand Clavier

Positif.

Cornet séparé.

Pedalle

G.C.

Positif.

30    *Mass for the Parishes*

# [XVI] Plainchant of the First Sanctus
## in Canon

[Grand Plein Jeu.
Péd.: Anches 8-4.]

Plein jeu.

Pedalle une octave plus bas.

Pedalle une octave plus bas.

# [XVII] *Récit de Cornet*

## (2nd Sanctus)

# [XVIII] Benedictus
## *Cromorne en Taille*

G.O.: Bourdon 8. Prestant 4.
P.: Cromorne.
Péd.: Flûte 8.

Fond d'orgue.

Pedalle de flute

Chromhorne.

# [XIX] Plainchant of the Agnus Dei
## alternately *en Basse* and *en Taille*

# [XX] Dialogue on the *Grands Jeux*
## (3rd Agnus)

G.O.: Bourdon 8, Prestant 4, Doublette 2,
Nasard, Tierce, Trompette.
P.: Cromorne, Prestant 4, Tierce.
R.: Cornet.
Péd.: Flûte 8-4.

## [XXI] Deo Gratias
### *Petit Plein Jeu*

FIN

# MASS FOR THE CONVENTS

*[Messe pour les Convents de Religieux
et Religieuses]*

(1690)

# [I] *Plein Jeu*
## (1st Kyrie)

[Petit Plein Jeu.]

49

# [II] Fugue on the *Trompette*
## (2nd Kyrie)

[G.O.: Bourdon 8, Prestant 4, Trompette.]

# [III] *Récit de Cromorne*

## (3rd Kyrie)

G.O.: Bourdon 8.
P.: Cromorne.

# [IV] Trio for Two Manuals
## on the *Cromorne* and the *Basse de Tierce*
### (4th Kyrie)

G.O.: Bourdon 8, Doublette, Nasard, Tierce.
P.: Cromorne.

# [V] Dialogue
## between the *Trompette* of the *Grand Clavier*
## and the *Montre*, *Bourdon* and *Nazard* of the *Positif*
### (5th and last Kyrie)

# [VI] *Plein Jeu*

## (Gloria, 1st verse)

[Grand Plein Jeu.]

## [VII] Little Fugue on the *Cromorne*

### (Gloria, 2nd verse)

[P.: Cromorne (Tierce ad lib.)]

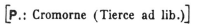

# [VIII] Duet on the *Tierces*

Gloria, 3rd verse)

G.O.: Bourdon 8, Flûte 4, Doublette, Nasard, Tierce.
P.: Bourdon 8, Nasard, Tierce.

# [IX] *Basse de Trompette*

## (Gloria, 4th verse)

Jeu doux.

Trompette.

# [X] *Cromorne sur la Taille*

## (Gloria, 5th verse)

P.: Cromorne.
G.O.: Bourdon 8, Prestant 4.
Péd.: Flûte 8.

Fond d'orgue.

Pedalle.

Chromhorne.

# [XI] Dialogue on the *Voix Humaine*
## (Gloria, 6th verse)

Voix humaine.

Jeu doux.

Jeu doux.

Voix hum.

Jeu doux.

Voix hum.

Jeu doux.

Voix hum.

Les 2 mains sur la Voix humaine.

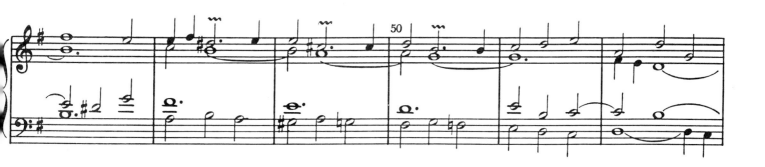

# [XII] Trio
## Upper voices on the *Tierce*
## and bass on the *Trompette*
### (Gloria, 7th verse)

G.O.: Trompette.
P.: Cornet décomposé.

# [XIII] *Récit de Tierce*

## (Gloria, 8th verse)

G.O.: Bourdon 8, Flûte 4.
  P.: Bourdon 8, Nasard, Doublette, Tierce.

# [XIV] Dialogue on the *Grands Jeux*

## (Gloria, last verse)

P.: Cromorne, Montre 4, Cornet.
G O.: Montre 8, Bourdon 16, Prestant 4, Doublette, Cornet, Trompette.

[Grand Clavier.]

# [XV] Offertory on the *Grands Jeux*

G.O.: Montre 8, Prestant 4, Doublette 2, Plein Jeu, Cornet, Trompette.
P.: Bourdon 8, Prestant 4, Nasard, Tierce, Cromorne.

# [XVI] First Sanctus
## *Plein Jeu*

# [XVII] *Récit de Cornet*

## (2nd Sanctus)

P.: Bourdon 8, Flûte 4.
G.O.: Cornet composé.

# [XVIII] Elevation
## *Tierce en Taille*

P.: Bourdon 8, Prestant 4.
G.O.: Cornet décomposé.
Péd.: Flûte 8.

Fond d'orgue.

Tierce.

Pedalle.

# [XIX] Agnus Dei
## *Plein Jeu*

[Petit Plein Jeu.]

# [XX] Dialogue on the *Grands Jeux*
## (Conclusion of the Agnus Dei)

G.O.: Montre 8, Prestant 4, Cornet décomposé, Trompette.
P.: Bourdon 8, Montre 4, Doublette, Nasard, Tierce, Cromorne.

Grand Clavier.

Grand Clavier.

[Positif.]

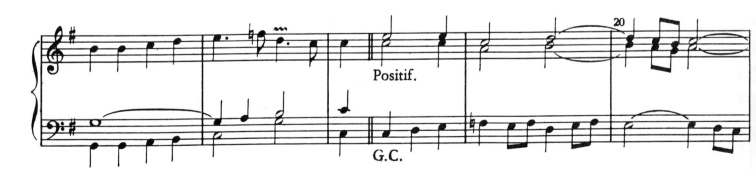

Positif.

G.C.

Les 2 mains sur le G.C.

# [XXI] Deo Gratias
## *Petit Plein Jeu*

THE END